D0574895

HELEN HALL LIBRARY
City of League City
100 West Walker
League City, TX 77573-3899

JUN 09

WORLD OF INSECTS

Ants

by Emily K. Green

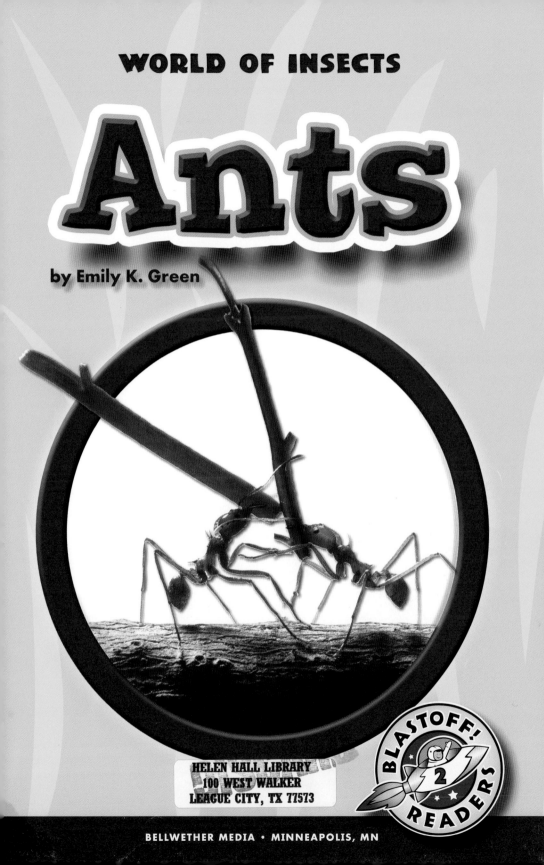

HELEN HALL LIBRARY
100 WEST WALKER
LEAGUE CITY, TX 77573

BLASTOFF!
2
READERS

BELLWETHER MEDIA • MINNEAPOLIS, MN

Note to Librarians, Teachers, and Parents:

Blastoff! Readers are carefully developed by literacy experts and combine standards-based content with developmentally appropriate text.

Level 1 provides the most support through repetition of high-frequency words, light text, predictable sentence patterns, and strong visual support.

Level 2 offers early readers a bit more challenge through varied simple sentences, increased text load, and less repetition of high-frequency words.

Level 3 advances early-fluent readers toward fluency through increased text and concept load, less reliance on visuals, longer sentences, and more literary language.

Whichever book is right for your reader, Blastoff! Readers are the perfect books to build confidence and encourage a love of reading that will last a lifetime!

This edition first published in 2007 by Bellwether Media.

No part of this publication may be reproduced in whole or in part without written permission of the publisher. For information regarding permission, write to Bellwether Media Inc., Attention: Permissions Department, Post Office Box 1C, Minnetonka, MN 55345-9998.

Library of Congress Cataloging-in-Publication Data
Green, Emily K., 1966-
  Ants / by Emily K. Green.
    p. cm. — (Blastoff! readers) (World of insects)
Summary: "Simple text accompanied by full-color photographs give an up-close look at ants."
  Includes bibliographical references and index.
  ISBN-10: 1-60014-008-4 (hardcover : alk. paper)
  ISBN-13: 978-1-60014-008-2 (hardcover : alk. paper)
  1. Ants—Juvenile literature. I. Title. II. Series. III. Series: Green, Emily K., 1966- World of insects.

  QL568.F7G684 2007
  595.79'6—dc22   2006009507

Text copyright © 2007 by Bellwether Media.
Printed in the United States of America.

Table of Contents

Ants are busy **insects**.

Ants can be many colors.
Most ants are black, brown,
or red.

Ants have smooth bodies.

waist

Ants have a skinny **waist**.

antennas

Ants have **antennas**. Their antennas bend.

Ants use their antennas to touch and smell.

All ants have six legs. Each
leg has a sharp **claw**.

jaws

Ants have strong **jaws**.

Ants use their jaws to eat.
Most ants eat plants or
other insects.

Ants use their jaws to dig.
Most ants dig a nest under
the ground.

13

Ants dig tunnels and rooms
in their nest.

Many ants make a **mound**
on top of their nest.

Ants live in a group called a **colony**.

16

Every colony has a **queen**.
The queen is bigger than
the other ants.

Ants leave the nest to find food. They walk in a line.

Ants work together to carry food back to the nest.

Ants are very strong.

They can carry objects that weigh more than they do. Good work!

Glossary

antennas—the long, thin feelers on an insect's head

claws—the sharp pinchers on the end of an ant's legs

colony—a group of ants that live together; an ant colony can have just a few ants or it can have millions of ants.

insect—a kind of animal that has a hard body; most insects also have two antennas, six legs, and two or four wings.

jaws—the sharp pinchers at the front of an ant's head

mound—a pile of sand or dirt at the opening of an ant's nest

queen—a female ant; the queen is the largest ant in the colony and the only ant that can have young.

waist—the skinny place in the middle of an ant's body

To Learn More

AT THE LIBRARY

Allen, Judy. *Are You an Ant?* New York: Kingfisher, 2002.

Climo, Shirley. *The Little Red Ant and the Great Big Crumb.* New York: Clarion Books, 1995.

Hoose, Phillip and Hannah. *Hey, Little Ant.* Berkeley, Calif.: Tricycle Press, 1998.

Pinczes, Elinor. *One Hundred Hungry Ants.* Boston: Houghton Mifflin, 1993.

Ryden, Hope. *ABC of Crawlers and Flyers.* New York: Clarion Books, 1996.

ON THE WEB

Learning more about ants is as easy as 1, 2, 3.

1. Go to www.factsurfer.com

2. Enter "ants" into search box.

3. Click the "Surf" button and you will see a list of related web sites.

With factsurfer.com, finding more information is just a click away.

Index

The photographs in this book are reproduced through the courtesy of: Tim Flach/Getty Images, front cover, pp. 5, 20; Mark Moffet/Getty Images, p. 4; Ismael Montero Verdu, p. 5(inset); Charles Kreb/Getty Images, p. 6; Chartchai Meesangnin, pp. 7, 9, 17; Chris Prior/Getty Images, p. 8; Johner/Getty Images, p. 10; David Maitland/Getty Images, pp. 11, 12; Heinrich van den Berg/Getty Images, p. 13; Dwight Kuhn Photography, p. 14; EM Designs, p. 15; Pat Coughlin, p. 15(inset); Hans Christian Heap/Getty Images, p. 16; Hans Neleman, p. 18; Hung Meng Tan, p. 19; Brian Mullennix, p. 21.